Gay, or Gifted?

Forgive Us Our Ignorance

Introduction

Over the course of the last several decades, many things have changed in our Western society. Our culture is changing and evolving every day. Beliefs are challenged as a revised moral landscape continues to spread over our country. Many things that were not acceptable in years past have become commonplace today. In American society, we have made several positive changes. However, we are still yet plagued with bigotry, racism, and other moral dilemmas that continue to erode the moral fabric of our society. One of the most heated topics continues to be a persons individual sexuality. Homosexuality versus heterosexuality has touched millions of families in America. Gay rights continue to be an issue in many states. Same-sex marriage is practiced in some states, while other states continue to resist this type of marriage. One thing is certain, this issue is not going to go away. There are always going to be individuals who struggle with their sexuality, as well as those who judge others because their beliefs do not mirror their own.

How does someone go about writing a book on the topic of homosexuality? No matter what is written, someone will take issue. (No matter how much it gets spelled out in the introduction that the book is intended to help, **not to harm**...to enlighten, **not to judge**....to provide hope, **not to condemn**...and to challenge people to to take a hard look at themselves, and not so much at others). The book *is* meant however, to open up the eyes of both homosexuals and heterosexuals regarding the divine purpose of certain individuals.

This book is **not for everyone**. It is not for the close minded or dogmatic religious person. In America, we each have the right to choose for ourselves what we believe to be right or wrong. Freedom of choice and freedom of religious belief are part of what makes this country great. We have the freedom to be closed-minded or open-minded. It is my sincerest hope, that by reading this book, certain individuals will open their eyes to what God has purposed for them. Through faith and trust in Him, the truth of His word might help them fulfill their *divine destiny*....realizing just how special they truly are in the eyes of God, and how great their divine calling actually is. It is also my hope that those who in past times have been critical or judgemental toward members of the homosexual community, after reading this book, might themselves learn to look at these men and women differently.

Finally, before starting this book, each reader should be aware that it is this author's sincere belief that every person has a purpose for being here; and that there is **one** sovereign and loving God who created each of us with that purpose.....a divine destiny. Also, that every person has been given gifts and talents intended to enable them to fulfill that destiny. Unfortunately, many individuals will never fulfill their God-given destiny. In fact, many are not even aware that one exists for them. With all of the evil, hatred, and horrible things that happen every day, it makes it difficult to believe that God is even real...let alone cares enough to have provided a wonderful plan for our lives. Yet God, and His love for us, is real. Whether or not we choose to believe He has a plan for us does not set aside the truth that He has indeed gifted each of us with something...and that something is intended to help us fulfill a divine destiny.

Some people *ARE* **born different from others**, but they have a destiny as well! They certainly do not deserve to be judged or *treated differently* because of their *differences*. In this book, I will discuss some reasons for being born differently, and cover the seldom talked about guidelines for judging others.

Chapter Outline:

Chapter 1

Now, More Than Ever

It is not easy to collect accurate data with regards to the gay, lesbian, bi-sexual and transgender community (the LGBT community). Although many more people feel more comfortable today letting the world know they are gay, there are also many still who do not. This makes getting accurate numbers difficult. Also, statistics will always vary when dealing with controversial topics. If you talk to the conservative left, the numbers will be smaller. If you speak with the liberal right, the numbers will be bigger. By researching several different sources, one could reasonably estimate about 1.7% of the American population are gay or lesbian. The latest U.S. Census Bureau shows more than 325 million Americans as of December 2016. Mathematically therefore, this means about 5.5 million people in America are gay or lesbian. According to the Williams Institute UCLA School of Law, another 1.8% of the American population claims to be bisexual and another 700,000 (0.002%) claim to be transsexual or transgender. This gives us a total of about 3.6% of the population making up the LGBT community here in America, or a little over 11.7 million. One would certainly think that from the amount of attention the media places on gay rights and on events that center around the gay and lesbian community, that this number would be much higher. These numbers are of course on the increase as more and more persons "come out of the closet" and society continues to increase it's acceptance of such persons.

This leads us to perhaps the most interesting statistic regarding the LGBT community. As of 2016, the Pew Research Center shows that 60% of Americans believe that homosexuality *is* acceptable, while only 37% of Americans believe that it *is not* acceptable behavior. (I did try very hard to find out what happened to the other 3% with no success. Maybe they had **no opinion** on the matter, or perhaps believed homosexuality was not a moral issue). As each year passes, the numbers of those who accept homosexual behavior are increasing. This means that we can ill afford to ignore the concerns and needs of the LGBT community.

As the number of gay and lesbian persons here in America continue to increase, it opens up more and more controversial issues to deal with. It is not just about an individual's sexuality anymore. What about marriage? Is it appropriate for two people of the same sex to get married? And what about adoption? Should gay and lesbian couples be allowed to adopt? According to the latest Gallup Poll, there are currently 780,000 gay or lesbian couples legally married in the United States. Gallup also lists 1.2 million other gay or lesbian couples in America who live together and claim each other as their significant other, or life partner. Accurate statistics for same-sex couples who have successfully adopted are difficult to find. Regardless of the overall numbers, these people *are* out there. They are *real* people with *real* feelings just like the rest of us. They are part of our community and we should not just label them as "twisted" and continue dismissing their issues.

There is a long-standing spiritual principle which states that any country, kingdom, group, or family that is divided against itself **will not stand**. Controversial issues like these above, and others, serve as instruments for the forces of darkness to divide. One of the greatest goals of Christianity is **unity.** Combined with the fact that as a *true* Christian one is encouraged to share his or her faith and help lead others to God, it makes it ***more important than ever*** that we should speak up and not run from these issues. Adversity often opens the door for opportunity. If we truly believe what we read in the Bible, and we truly believe heaven and hell are real, then we will want others to end up in heaven, not hell. (Especially if we care for someone!) **Now, more than ever**, it is important for us as a Christian country to address these controversial issues. We should speak out! Remaining silent will not solve anything. However, to achieve any measure of success in unifying our country, and our church as a whole, we need to do this *biblically...*in a way that the Lord Jesus Christ would approve. We cannot achieve our goals by violating the very principles which Christianity stands for: love, forgiveness, patience, and gentleness. If we ever hope to share the light of God with others, **that light must first shine in us.**

Chapter 2

Here We Go

In order to move forward, it is necessary to cover the Scriptures that pertain to homosexuality. Although it is **not the goal of this book** to convince anyone that homosexual behavior is a sin, it is necessary to establish a baseline from which the rest of the book may be written. These Scriptures *are* in the Bible for a reason, and if the Bible is truly God's word (which this writer believes unconditionally) then we each have a responsibility to decide what to do with these, and all, the verses of the Bible. True Christians should not treat the Bible like a box of chocolates, picking out the ones they like, while discarding the ones they don't.

In the Old Testament, there are only two verses that directly address homosexual behavior. These are both found in Leviticus: 18:22: "You shall not lie with a male as you lie with a female: it is an abomination" and 20:13: "If any man lies with a male as he lies with a female, both of them has committed an abomination..." (both New American Standard Bible) There is also of course the account in Genesis chapters 18 and 19 regarding Abraham's nephew Lot, and his nightmare in Sodom and Gomorrah. While no one disputes that the men of Sodom and Gomorrah were desiring sex with other men, it is interesting to note that God did not condemn these cities because of homosexual behavior...although these two cities will be brought up by those condemning homosexuality. God however, speaking through the prophet Ezekiel in chapter 18:49, states that the sin of Sodom and Gomorrah was actually

"...pride, the fullness of bread (prosperity), and abundance of idleness (laziness)..." (King James Version...parenthesis mine).

In the New Testament, homosexuality is mentioned in Romans 1:26 and 27, 1st Corinthians 6:9, and 1st Timothy 1:10. The verses in Romans talk about both sexes leaving their "natural" purpose. One needs only to look at creation, specifically the other animals, to understand that the Creator made them male and female...and that these two are biologically designed to come together and reproduce. Human beings of course have the right to resist God's natural plan, but that does not negate the fact that it's still wrong to do so, and that there will be consequences. If a bird decides to resist it's God given instinct to fly south during the winter...it will likely die.

In 1st Corinthians 6:9 the Apostle Paul asks, "Don't you know that the unrighteous will not inherit God's kingdom? Do not be deceived: No sexually immoral people, idolaters, adulterers, or anyone practicing homosexuality" (Holman Christian Standard Bible). Paul also writes in 1st Timothy 1:10, "for the sexually immoral, for those practicing homosexuality, for slave traders and liars and perjurers--and for whatever else is contrary to the sound doctrine" (New International Version). The Greek word used in these two verses is *arsenokoitais*, and is properly translated into English as "practicing homosexual behavior". Aside from the obvious, one should notice here that God is dealing with practicing behaviors. Yes, homosexuality is a behavior. (Chapter 6 of this book will deal with the biology of human gender). Also, understand that these two verses are dealing with persons who are **actively practicing** the behavior....not someone who has had a previous encounter and *discontinued* the practice.

It is interesting to note, that out of the **several hundred Bible verses** addressing human conduct which God considers sinful, only five envolve homosexual behavior. One would think that there would be more, especially considering the amount of attention that this particular topic generates. This does not set aside God's assertion that this behavior is considered sinful of course, but it does seem to tell us that this is just one of *many* other behaviors that need to be dealt with in order to have a *right* relationship with Him.

Understanding the culture during the time of the writings could also provide some explanation as to why there are only a few verses. Homosexual behavior, although present during Bible times, wasn't largely practiced and was considered morally wrong by the masses. One could conclude therefore, that it wasn't necessary to spend time in the Scriptures convincing people that this type of behavior was wrong. One had only to look at nature, and observe the breeding habits of animals to understand that the Creator's plan has always been for a male and a female to mate...this is how procreation is accomplished. Some will say at this point, "if God is truly a God of love, how can He condemn me for loving my partner?" My answer to this would be simply, "I am sure that heroin addicts love to get high, but that doesn't mean that it's lawful, or not sinful". Please understand, God loves **all people**...even those engaged in sinful behavior. However, He does not love **all behaviors**. God hates sin, not the sinner. "For God so loved the world, that he gave his only begotten Son, that whosoever believeth in him shall not perish, but have everlasting life...for God sent not his Son into the world to condemn the world; but that the world through him might be saved" John 3:16, 17 (King James Version).

Chapter 3

Judge, Jury, Executioners

Christian or not, most people are passionate about something. Generally, the more someone *genuinely cares* about a particular something, the more passionate that person is going to be about it...especially when discussing it with others. As a Christian, we have a responsibility to help others and share our faith. Jesus did commission His followers to go into all the world and share their faith. Many Christians display great zeal and a strong desire to help lead others to Christ. Unfortunately however, many times their zeal is not tempered with wisdom. The kind of wisdom which comes from reading God's word and learning *when it is* appropriate to speak to someone, and *when it is not*. Often times, in attempting to lead homosexuals to Christ, one becomes judgemental. The Bible has a great deal to say about judging. In this chapter, we will examine some Biblical guidelines concerning the sharing of ones faith, and what the Bible says about judging others.

It is necessary to point out at this time, that different parts of the Bible are addressed to different groups. Certain scriptures are written specifically to Christians *only*, while other parts of the Bible are written for all mankind...whether believer or nonbeliever. The verses which deal with judging others fall under this criteria. For example, the commonly recognized verses in Matthew chapter 7 regarding judging others are written to *everyone*, and are intended to be a **general guideline** for healthy human relationships. Matthew 7:1 reads, "Do not Judge, so that you will not be judged." Verse two goes on to say, "For in the way you judge, you will be judged; and by your standard of measure, it will be measured to you". (New American Standard Bible, both) In many instances, verse 1 is quoted in defense by someone who is being confronted about something *perceived by the person doing the confronting* as wrong, or sinful. Verse 2 does not get quoted nearly as much, but it certainly goes together well with verse 1. It tells us plainly that the standard we hold others to, **will be the same standard God holds us to!**

Just as there are verses in the Bible which tell us not to judge, there **are** also verses in the Bible that plainly instruct us "*to judge*". These verses however, unlike the verses mentioned above, are written to a specific audience and are **not** intended for everyone. Christians are instructed to **only judge other Christians**, and even then, only when there is irrefutable evidence concerning the behavior in question. Christians are specifically instructed **not to judge nonbelievers**. The apostle Paul makes both points clear in 1st Corinthians chapter 5. He instructs *the brethren* to not only judge the fellow believer practicing sexual immorality, but he goes on to instruct the believers there to actually **separate themselves** from him (verses 5 and 9). Paul goes on to say in verse 12 that it is none of his business to judge outsiders (nonbelievers, those outside the church body) only those inside the body (believers). In verse 13 he states that it is God's responsibility to judge nonbelievers, not Christians! Paul also writes in Galations 6:1: "Dear brothers and sisters, if another believer is overcome by some sin, you who are godly should gently and humbly help that person back onto the right path. And be careful not to fall into the same temptation yourself. " (New Living Translation) Jesus teaches His disciples in John 7:24 to "Judge not according to appearance, but judge righteous judgement." (King James Version). The message here is straight forward...get your facts straight before drawing conclusions...appearances can be deceiving. Chapter 6 of this book will discuss certain individuals who for biological reasons, appear different *outwardly* (physically) from what they actually are *inwardly* (genetically).

Perhaps the most *disregarded* guideline concerning the judgement of others is recorded in Matthew chapter 7, verses 3-5: "And why do you look at the speck that is in your brother's eye, but do not notice the log that is in your own eye? Or how can you say to your brother, 'Let me take the speck out of your eye,' and behold, the log is in your own eye? You hypocrite, first take the log out of your own eye, and then you will see clearly to take the speck out of your brother's eye" (New American Standard) One wonders how many people, who openly speak out and condemn homosexual behavior, have dirty laundry themselves? Obviously, proof of just how much this goes on is difficult, because most folks are not generally eager to divulge their own hidden sins.

It is interesting to think about the irony created by hypocritical people who speak out against homosexuality. It is the same God that they are *supposedly* standing up for when they speak out, that knows the contents of *their* heart, and will ultimately end up judging them! They may be able to hide their closet skeletons from others, but they are not going to hide them from God. There is nothing hidden from God (Hebrews 4:13) and He knows the contents of **all** human hearts (Jeremiah 17:10). It is sad to think about the fact that the person holding up the protest sign condemning homosexuality, could likely be going home to sneak a peek at pornography on his (or her) computer, or "pig out" at the dinner table...further adding to his or her already gluttonous waistline.

Sin is not the only thing hidden in the human heart that will disqualify someone from making judgments. The ***motive for speaking out must also be pure.*** Motive is the "why" we do things...the real reason behind what we are doing or saying. In 1st Corinthians 16:14, Paul writes to believers... "Let all that you do be done in love". (New American Standard Bible) **Love is the motive** that God intends all believers to operate in. It is difficult to operate in love however, with a guilty conscience. A large number of people in churches today are not happy with themselves on the *inside*. Even though they go to church and *claim* to know Jesus, hidden sins and other personal issues that have not been dealt with, have defiled their consciences. Outwardly they appear alright, but inwardly they have a problem. (Just because someone goes to church, that does make them a **true** Christian....no more than walking into a garage makes one a car). The Pharisees had this problem. (The Pharisees were one of the major religious groups during Jesus's lifetime). They were very judgemental of others, particularly those involved in sexual sins. Jesus addresses their hypocrisy in Matthew chapter 23:27, 28 by saying, "Woe to you, scribes and Pharisees, you hypocrites! You are like whitewashed tombs, which look beautiful on the outside, but on the inside are full of dead men's bones and every impurity...in the same way, you appear to be righteous on the outside, but on the inside you are full of hypocrisy and wickedness" (Berean Study Bible) The Pharisees were certainly **not** motivated by love.

Unfortunately, there are many *religious* people today who act exactly the same way...particularly towards those of the gay and lesbian community! They become judge, jury, and executioners for anyone practicing homosexuality. For these *so called believers*, the only way to take the attention away from their own guilt is to try to point the finger at someone else. For them, the only way to feel better on the inside about themselves is to criticize others.

In summary, an entire book could be dedicated to the topic of judging others. Hopefully, this chapter brings an awareness to both believers and nonbelievers that proper guidelines exist, and that these guidelines need to be followed before making *any* judgment. If someone claims to be a Christian, then they should follow the rules outlined in the Bible. Ultimately, God alone is the judge of all mankind, and we will each give an account of ourselves before Him. God certainly did not commission believers to pin sheriff badges on their chests, and go around "fixing" other peoples' *perceived* problems. It is actually grieving to think about the damage that is done by well-meaning Christians who simply are not following the guidelines that God provided for them.

Chapter 4

The Revelation

One of the strongest counter statements used by persons engaged in homosexual activity is that they are feeling judged for being **who they truly are.** One young man I personally spoke with, told me that from his earliest memory, "He has always felt different," and that "He *knew from childhood,*" he was different. Perhaps some of you have heard these questions asked: "How could God say that what I am doing is wrong, if **He** made me this way?" and "Why would God make me like this, and then judge me for it?" Unfortunately, the answers to these questions have often sounded something like this: "God did *not* make you that way...homosexuality is a choice...and you are choosing to be that way." This type of reply begs the obvious question, "How can *anyone* tell someone else what they are, or are not, feeling in their *own* heart...in their own spirit?" One wonders how many homosexuals have been told (by *well meaning* people) that they are simply "making excuses" in order to justify their own lustful desires? It is my personal and sincere belief, that many of the individuals who say that they have always felt *different* are **telling the absolute truth**. In *some* instances, there **are** medical explanations...which I will discuss in chapter 6. In this chapter however, I will discuss one explanation *I believe* to be true; and, provide *biblical reasons* for this belief. In all of my 26 years as a Christian, I have never heard the following offered as an explanation regarding a person's feeling different sexually from his or her earliest memories. Nor, have I ever heard any Christian minister, pastor, or believer ever discuss the following Scriptures in the manner that will be discussed in this chapter. For many, it will truly be a *revelation.*

The Bible verses that we will be examining come from the Gospel of Matthew, chapter 19. Here, Jesus is with His disciples ministering in His homeland of Judea. A great multitude of people were following Him and throngs of people were rushing out to meet Him. The Pharisees (the religious group discussed in the previous chapter of this book) also came out to meet Him. The Pharisees were very jealous of Jesus's ministry and popularity. They perceived Him to be a threat to their position and power. In this account, they asked a controversial question from the Jewish Law of Moses regarding divorce, in an attempt to trip Him up in front of the people. In Matthew 19:3 asked Jesus, "is it lawful for a man to divorce his wife for any reason?" (Berean Study Bible) Jesus responded in verses 4 through 6, "Have you not read that He who made them from the beginning made them male and female, and said, for this cause shall a man leave his father and mother, and shall cling to his wife; and the two shall become one flesh? So that there are no longer two, but one flesh. What therefore God has joined together, let not man put asunder" (American Standard Version). The Pharisees **obviously** didn't like His answer. They proceeded to ask Jesus in verse 7, "Why then did Moses order a man to give his wife a certificate of divorce and send her away?" (Berean Study Bible) Jesus replied in verses 8 and 9: "Because of your hardness of heart Moses allowed you to divorce your wives, but from the beginning it was not so. I tell you that whoever divorces his wife, except for sexual immorality, and marries another, commits adultery. And he who marries her when she is divorced, commits adultery." (New Heart English Bible) **Please understand that it is not the purpose of this book to talk about marriage or divorce!** There are plenty of other books out there that can be read on those subjects. For the purpose of this book however, we do need to understand that Jesus's response was **not what the Pharisees wanted to hear,** and it was definitely not what *anyone* expected.

Jesus' reply not only upset the Pharisees, but all those around who heard His words, including His own disciples. Keep in mind that up to this point in the Jewish culture, divorce was easy and commonplace (reminds me of America). The disciples had been with Jesus for more than two years at this point in His ministry. They knew from personal experience, that whatever Jesus said was true...so they received what He had just said about marriage and divorce, drawing from it an interesting conclusion. In Matthew 19:10 His disciples came to Him and said, "If this is the case of a husband with a wife, it is better not to marry!" (New English Translation). You can just imagine some of their thoughts: "Wow, God expects me to stay married for better or for worse? or maybe wondered something like this: "As long as she doesn't cheat on me, I have to stay married?" The answer is "yes" to both questions. How can we know this? Simple: Jesus' reply in Matthew 19:11 *agrees* with their conclusion...and **this is what leads us to the main purpose for writing this book, and one answer to why certain homosexuals have always felt different regarding their sexuality.**

In Matthew 19:11 and 12, Jesus uses His disciples statement as an opportunity to unveil a ***revelation***...*for a **select few**, celibacy is the result of a very special **gift** granted to them **from God**.* (Celibate means to be sexually inactive) Jesus responded to His disciples by saying in Matthew 19:11,12: "All *men* cannot receive this saying, except they to whom it is given. For there are some eunuchs, which were born so from their mothers womb: and there are some eunuchs, which were made eunuchs by men: and there are eunuchs which have made themselves eunuchs for the kingdom of heaven's sake. He that is able to receive it, let him receive *it* " (King James Version). (Side note, in the original Greek writings, the word "men" is **not there** in verse 11, which means these two verses apply to both men and women. This makes perfect sense because *God does **not** discriminate* between men and women, *people **do***). Here, Jesus agrees with His disciples that it is actually ***not*** good to marry, but that this "saying" (the disciples conclusion from verse 10) *cannot be received by everyone*, only to whom it has been **"given"** or granted. Jesus then goes on in Matthew 19:12 to teach about eunuchs. A eunuch is someone who (for varying reasons) does not participate in sexual activity...they are *celibate*. We learn in this verse that there are actually **three** types, or categories, of eunuchs in the world. Let's take a look at each of them in *reverse* order.

Jesus stated in verse 12 quoted above that there are eunuchs who "have made themselves eunuchs for the kingdom of heaven's sake". This is a person who for the sake of the kingdom of God has *chosen* to be celibate. Examples of this are Catholic nuns and priests. They (both men and women) have taken a ***vow** of celibacy* as part of their ministry for God. They have made a choice. This **does not mean** that they do not *have* sexual desires; it simply means that they have chosen, of their own free will, to not move forward *on* those desires. Trying to *deny* ones sexual desires is a huge mistake. It is certainly heartbreaking that we hear so much about sexual abuse among the priesthood. I am certainly **not an expert** on the Catholic faith, or the prior training required to become a nun or priest. However, I would certainly expect that anyone desiring to enter this type of ministry would be made **fully** aware that dealing with his or her **sexual desires** will be an on-going challenge and responsibility. This type of eunuch **has** hormones that produce a sex drive. However, he or she *chooses to suppress* these desires, and not participate in sexual activity. One might ask at this point, "Why would anyone want to do this? or "What advantage is there in being celibate? We will discuss this a little later in this chapter. For now, let's look at the next type of eunuch.

The second category of eunuch that Jesus mentioned in Matthew 19:12 are those eunuchs "which have been made eunuchs by men". This particular category applies only to men. These men do not participate in sex because they **have no sex drive**. The reason they have no sex drive is because *other men* prevented them from developing one by having them castrated before they reach the age of puberty. (Yes, have their testicles cut off!) In many instances, these men were taken as servants or slaves during childhood. Without testicles, the human male cannot produce the necessary hormones (particularly testosterone) to develop a normal male sex drive. In short, they had **no libido**. (I *should note here* that female castration was possible during these times, but not for the purpose of preventing normal sexual hormonal development. During these times, in rare instances, the exterior female sex organs were cut off as *punishment*, or in an attempt to *prevent* her from being able to bare children. In the case of the latter, oftentimes it was unsuccessful).

Why was this done (male castration) you might ask? It was common practice in ancient times for men of royalty or wealth to have many ***beautiful*** wives. (Yes, they had harems). When these boys became adults they were often selected to guard these women. They were made eunuchs, so that they would **not be tempted to have sexual relations** with the women that they were guarding. It would be like having a security guard placed *inside* the womens' locker room today. It would be almost impossible for any man with a normal, **healthy sex drive** to avoid getting in trouble with these women. (Imagine watching dozens of beautiful women every day bathing and changing clothes right in front of you). The solution was to prevent them from *ever developing* a sex drive...this is why they were castrated and "made eunuchs by men".

The first category of eunuch which Jesus spoke about in verse 12 were, "Those who were born so from their mother's womb". The first word recorded in verse 12 is "for" or, "because". This ties the beginning of verse 12 to the last words used in Matthew 19:11, "to whom it is given", referring to **a gift from God given only to a select few.** Celibacy for this category of eunuch is not the result of a *vow* he or she has taken. Nor is it the result of having been *forcefully castrated* as a youth. It is the result of having been given a gift from God! This eunuch is **born this way**, and God is responsible for it. Most of you might say at this point, "Are you trying to tell me that there are certain individuals born in this world without normal sexual desires and attractions for the opposite sex?" and that "This is considered to be a gift from God?" Yes, that is exactly what I am saying on both points! This (eunuch) person, whether male or female, **was born to be celibate!**

Let's take a more detailed look at these two passages (Matthew 19:11, 12). In order to do this correctly, we need to remember that English versions of the Bible contain chapter and verse numerals which were inserted so that we can locate scriptures more quickly. Jesus' reply did not contain "11" and/or "12", and it should be examined as one *continuous* statement. Doing this helps us to understand these passages more clearly. It becomes evident from Jesus' statement that God has given something to this person which enables him or her to receive the "saying" spoken by the disciples in verse 10. The last word recorded in verse 11 is "given" or "granted". Let me ask "What is given or granted?" The answer: a *gift* (or perhaps a privilege). When one *combines* all of this, what is the conclusion? The conclusion is this: certain individuals have a God given *"gift"* **from birth** (verse 12). This *gift* results in him or her not wanting to be married (the saying from verse 10) and enables him or her to be sexually **inactive**...the 1st of the three types of eunuchs listed in verse 12). Furthermore, this *gift* is only intended for a select few (verse 11). Now, I am no doctor, nor am I a hormone specialist (although, I am married), but the only thing which could accomplish all this is some type of physiological/biological ***difference*** which affects the way a person thinks. How exactly God accomplishes all of this (whether supernatural or chemical) I do not know, nor is it of any *primary* importance. It is the **outcome** here that is paramount, not the means by which it is accomplished.

Honestly, I would find all of this hard to believe except for the fact that the apostle **Paul had this gift himself** and wrote about it in 1st Corinthians chapter 7 (commonly referred to as *the marriage chapter*). In verse 7 of 1st Corinthians Paul says that he wished "all men" were like him, but each person "has their own gift from God". He goes on to say in verses 32 through 35 that it is better (if possible) not to marry because this would afford one the opportunity to serve God in ministry without distraction or anxiety. We all know that *being married adds stress.* Not having to devote time and resources to a spouse allows one to fully commit **all** of one's time and resources in serving the Lord.

From the context of Paul's writings, it would seem that this gift was/is rare. Why God would equip Paul with this type of gift is somewhat obvious. In 2nd Corinthians chapter 11, Paul shares with the believers at Corinth a lengthy list of insane trials he had gone through because of his ministry for the Lord. No one in their right mind would want to be married while going through those type of trials. It certainly would not be fair to the spouse either. (That list included being killed and raised by God).

From the Scriptures, we do know that Paul was celibate...and that he called it a "gift" from God. He also stated in the latter part of 1st Corinthians chapter 7 that marriage was *good* and there was no problem if a person wanted to get married, but if he or she wanted the absolute *best* for his or her ministry...remain single. Remaining single however, is not always easy. Especially if your hormones are racing and you want to have sexual relations. For **dedicated** Christians, the only way to have sexual relations is to be married...so the benefits of having this gift are rather **obvious.**

We have all heard at one time or another about a Christian minister, or pastor, that had his (or her) ministry destroyed because of some *sexual* misconduct. Sex scandals are in the news constantly. How many of these ministers who lost everything would jump at the chance to have the gift of celibacy? How many ministers would love to be able to stand behind the pulpit each week and *never* be tempted in the least by an attractive woman or man wearing a short skirt or tight pants? Living a life completely free of lust or sexual temptation is unimaginable for most. Equipped with *this gift* however, someone could be very effective in the ministry. In fact, I believe someone like this would not only be effective in their ministry, but *dynamic.* This person would definitely be a threat to the forces of darkness and the worldly systems which teach us that lust and selfish desires are fine, as long as they occur between consenting adults. I also strongly believe the person born with this gift would definitely be on the devil's radar.

Chapter 5

The Attack

After reading the previous chapter, many of you might think that having this gift would be great...**if called into the Christian ministry**...but what in the world does this gift have to do with homosexuals? The answer is not such a stretch, and it is another important reason for writing this book. I am certain that **some** of the individuals out there who are practicing homosexuality, and who know with certainty that from their earliest memories they were different (having no sexual desires), *are actually called by God to be one of His greatest weapons against the forces of darkness*. Yes, there are those who become homosexuals *not because they are truly attracted to members of the same sex*, but because the devil has robbed them of their destiny *and* **twisted** *their God-given gift into something it was not intended to be.*

Having this gift means having to deal with the devil (yes, **the devil is real**...and so are his demons). One cannot believe in angels and God, and not believe in demons and the devil...they go together. Satan (another Biblical name for the devil) and his demons **cannot** allow these elite soldiers, chosen by God and equipped with this amazing gift, to fulfill their destiny. He is going to do everything within his power to prevent these individuals from ever receiving what God has intended for them. He will stop at nothing in preventing these individuals from ever learning the truth. Jesus teaches in John 8:32 that "knowing the truth sets you free". Satan also knows the Scriptures. Since the Garden of Eden he has twisted the truth and spun lies in order to undermine God's plans. Jesus calls satan the father of all lies (John 8:44), and the best lie is usually one that has *elements of the truth* woven throughout it.

Yes, it is *true* that these select few *are* different. Yes, it is *true* that these individuals have *never* been sexually attracted to the opposite sex. And yes, it is *true* that they are *not* like other people. However, they are **not** this way because they are homosexual...*that's the lie!* Furthermore (some more truth), the reason *these* select individuals are like this is **not** because they were born the *wrong sex,* it is because they were given *this gift of celibacy* from God! (There are those who are born sexually ambiguous. This will be discussed in the following chapter). This gift is *intended* to make them different, *intended* to make them more focused than the average person, and *intended* to help them achieve greatness in the kingdom of God! Because of this gift these individuals are very special, and a *severe threat* to the devil and his agenda! He has no choice but to *attack* them.

Jesus states in John 10:10 that Satan's desire, or goal, is to "rob, kill, and destroy". In Mark 4:15, Jesus teaches that Satan comes *immediately* to rob us of the truth that God is trying to plant in our heart. What better way for the devil to rob someone of his or her destiny and blind that person to the truth, **than to attack him or her as a child?** Children are especially innocent, and highly impressionable. What better way to undermine God's plan for them, than to "twist" the truth...by convincing them that *because* they have "no attraction" for the opposite sex they ***must*** be homosexual?

Imagine the peer pressure on a 12-year-old boy, or girl, who watches nearly all of his or her friends experiment with sex and begin to go on dates...but on the inside have *no desire him/herself* to participate? Think about all of those laugh filled conversations *you had back in school* about what so-and-so looked like in those ***cute*** blue jeans. Imagine being surrounded by all this sexual tension, but not "getting it" because on the inside you don't feel the same way. This person could care less about what the other kids are talking about because he or she has no attraction for the opposite sex. If this particular teenager has this God-given gift of celibacy, he or she does not have the standard sex hormones which begin raging at puberty. There is ***no doubt*** that this would create a great deal of **confusion.** Any teenager who felt like this would *want answers*. Being able to "fit in" is paramount for the average teenager. He or she would want to know "Why am I not like other teenagers?" Put this together with the average teenager's growing curiosity about the issues of life, and **bingo**...the stage is set! This is the opportunity the devil and his lying demons have been waiting for. The ground is young and furtile, just waiting for a "seed" to be planted. Satan is more than happy during this confusing time to plant one in this teenager's life.

Satan loves to whisper things in our ears. From childhood, I can remember cartoons depicting a little angel on one shoulder, and a little devil on the other. Each of them whispering in the ear of the person what *they* want him or her to do. One, the voice of good...the truth; the other, the voice of evil..the lie. Unfortunately, satan's seed **will** "twist" the truth. It will likely sound something like this: "If you are not attracted to the opposite sex, then *you must be attracted to the same sex*. The reason you are different is because **you are a homosexual!"** Think about this for a moment. After all, it *does* provide a **possible** explanation as to why they are different. Also keep in mind that in modern culture, if a person remains celibate their entire life, it is because there is something *wrong* with them. For Americans, a lifetime of celibacy is "not natural". We are taught in American culture (whether spoken out loud, or just silently understood to be this way), that each of us will grow up and find that "special" person...and when we do, we **will have sex** with them! We may, or may not, actually marry. This special someone may, or may not, be of the opposite sex. But eventually, *we all have sex with someone*! Not participating in sex for an entire lifetime, is not an option for the vast majority in American society. So you see, this seed offers these gifted teenagers a culturally perfect, and acceptable, explanation. The problem is however, "**This seed is a lie**!"

Although rare, there are accounts of former homosexuals who have shared how it all started for them. If you do not believe these people are out there, simply log-in to any search engine website and type the following phrase: "testimonies from former homosexuals". You will find page after page of websites filled with testimonies from *former* homosexuals opening up about their childhood. Hundreds of individuals have shared on the Internet their difficult sexual history, and how they came to believe they were homosexuals.

Some of these men and women were sexually abused as children, so opening up is especially difficult. It is not easy to openly share intimate details of our sex life anyway...but having been sexually abused makes it nearly impossible. Add to this, the fact that opening up **invites persecution**. (According to some recent internet statistics, approximately 40% of Americans believe that homosexuality is morally wrong). Fear of persecution from friends, family, and society is a very real and powerful thing. In the end, it makes it very difficult to know just how many practicing homosexuals felt this way on the inside when they were young, and *tricked* by the devil into believing that they were really homosexuals. Yet, there *are those* who have admitted this very thing.

In addition, others have admitted that the first time they had sex with a person of the same gender they were very, very uncomfortable. **Not** with the understandable nervousness that accompanies a person who is participating in sex for the first time with someone...but an uneasiness that goes far beyond. An uneasiness that was telling them *in their hearts* that what they were about to do was wrong. I have personally read testimonies from young individuals who stated that although they felt down inside homosexual behavior was wrong, they did it anyway! They admitted to **not** being attracted to this person sexually, but because they felt pressured, they had sex with them anyway (as if peer pressure had anything to do with teenage sexual activity...lol).

In our modern American culture, abstaining from sex as a teenager is considered *not* cool...even taboo! Interestingly, even though these individuals were "not feeling 100% comfortable" with what they had done...they went ahead and did it again...*and again!* Gradually, the little voice on the inside which was saying, "don't do this", faded away. For them, confusion is now replaced with understanding. Inner needs for love and acceptance are now being ***temporarily*** supplied through this homosexual relationship. Perhaps, for the first time in his or her life, this person begins to experience some type inner peace, and a sense of belonging. All this person *knows* is that from childhood, he or she has always felt different. He or she had never experienced inner peace or a sense of true belonging...until receiving and acting on satan's lying seed. After studying all of this, and learning the truth, it is easy to understand why satan's lie has been so effective at deceiving these gifted individuals. But what about the ones who have medical reasons for being different?

Chapter 6

The Biology

As previously noted, one of the goals of this book is to present **one** possible explanation "Biblically" as to why certain homosexuals have always felt that they were born differently...why they *knew* there was something "sexually" about them which made them feel different from the average person. It would take an entire volume of books to cover *all* of the *possible* explanations; however, I do believe that it is necessary to briefly cover (in this book) *some* of the ***biological*** reasons. Let me state at this point, that **I am no expert in the medical field whatsoever.** I am ***not*** a doctor or a child psychologist, ***nor*** do I claim to be an *expert* in human biology or genetics. Thanks to the internet however, the information in this chapter is available to everyone.

There **are** very real physiological conditions which affect gender identity and sexual preference. As I stated, ***some*** of these will be discussed in this chapter. The average person has very little knowledge of these conditions (assuming he or she even knows these conditions exist). Partially because of this ignorance, individuals to which this chapter applies, have also been wrongly judged. (I say "partially" because sadly, there are people out there who would judge these individuals even if they knew all about their medical issues) Just as the information in chapter 4 applies to only a small portion of the LGBT community, so too, the information in this chapter applies only to a small portion of the LGBT community. However, there are very real medical explanations why some individuals grow up feeling different, believing perhaps that they are the wrong sex. For some, these biological conditions also provide a possible answer as to why they feel that they are attracted to the same sex. **These conditions need to be talked about!** As will be discussed later in this chapter, secrecy, and "not talking about it" only adds *further psychological problems* to these biological conditions. This chapter will only *scratch the surface* of what **could** be talked about...but it *should* provide a basic understanding for the average individual.

Genetically, the sex of a child is determined **at conception**. The female's egg cell contains an "X" chromosome, while the male's sperm cell contains either an "X" or a "Y" chromosome. These chromosomes determine the child's sex...*genetically*. **Normally**, an embryo inherits one pair of sex chromosomes; one "X" from the mother, and either one "X" or one "Y" from the father. The genetic sex of the child is *determined by the father*. If the egg receives an X chromosome from the father, the baby will be female. If the egg receives a Y chromosome from the father, the baby will be male.

The male and female reproductive organs and genitals both come from the same tissue in the fetus. Sexually, both the male and female embryos develop **identically**, and have the **same gonads and genital parts**, until about the *eighth week* of pregnancy. At that point, the embryo begins to develop distinct sexual characteristics. For **boys,** the internal genital tissue transforms into the prostate gland and vas deferens. The gonads turn into testes which begin producing male sex hormones (including testosterone). These male hormones allow the penis and scrotum to develop. For **girls,** the internal genital tissue transforms into the uterus, fallopian tubes, and the vagina. The gonads turn into ovaries which begin producing female sex hormones (including estrogen). The absence of male hormones is *vital* for the female genitalia to develop properly.

Because the physical sexual parts for both males and females develop from the same fetal tissue, and share this same fetal tissue for the first eight weeks of development, *it is possible* for an infant's sex *"physically"* to differ from it's sex *"genetically"*. Yes, outwardly an infant can *appear* to be a *male*, but on the inside, **genetically**, the infant is *actually female…or vice a versa!* "Wow, how could *this* happen?" one might ask. During the first eight weeks, if any disruption in the embryo's natural development occurs, it can cause *birth defects* which hinder normal sexual development. Specifically, if the normal process that causes this fetal tissue to become "male" or "female" is altered, or disrupted, in *ANY* way...**ambiguous genitalia** can develop. Ambiguous genitalia is a birth defect of the sex organs that makes it unclear whether an affected newborn is a girl or boy. If *severe* ambiguous genitalia develops, it makes it difficult to identify the infant's sex, *physically*. In some *rare* instances, the infant's physical appearance may fully develope **opposite** to the infant's genetic sex.

Some of these defects are caused by hormonal imbalances. If a fetus develops too much or too little of certain hormones, it will affect how the baby's genitals develop. Most people have heard of *testosterone* and *estrogen*, but there are other hormones involved in sexual development such as "cortisol" and "androgen". Imbalances in these hormones can cause sexual abnormalities to occur in babies. According to the Intersex Society of America, as of 2016 *one in every 1500* babies are born with *some type* of sexual ambiguity. The extent of the ambiguity can vary from girls having more masculine characteristics or vice versa, to babies born sexually **indeterminate** (a term used to describe babies whose sex cannot be determined at birth).

Genetic testing can determine if the child is a genetic male or female. Examining certain cells is often enough to determine the genetic sex of the infant. But what about the sex of the child physically? Until just a few years ago, the word used to identify (or label) these type of infants was *intersex.* In the modern medical community, the term "intersex" has been discarded in favor of a more neutral sounding "disorders of sex development" or *DSD*. Most individuals have never heard of either. Perhaps some of you have heard the word "hermaphrodite". *True hermaphroditism* is a rare condition in which tissue from both the ovaries and testicles is present. The child may also have parts of *both male and female genitalia*. Hermaphroditism is a type of DSD. There are several other types of sexual abnormalities which are categorized as DSD, but trying to discuss all of them would open up *Pandora's box*. However, this *does explain* why *some* members of the LGBT community have felt that they were born different regarding their sexual identity.

Ambiguous genitalia is usually not life-threatening. However, it usually creates huge *emotional and psychological issues* for the child, and difficult social problems for both the child and family. Place yourself for a moment in this situation. Can you imagine having a child which the doctors cannot tell you whether it is a boy or girl? What do you do? There are a wide range of factors which could determine a baby's sex. Ultimately, the sex chosen for an intersex (DSD) baby is the one doctors and the child's family believe he or she will grow up to identify with the best. What happens however, if they choose wrong?

Sometimes *surgery* is "medically" necessary, but in many instances, parents **choose** surgery for their baby. (Interestingly, there is a growing movement today against these surgeries). For this reason, a team of **experienced** specialists, including neonatologists, geneticists, endocrinologists, and psychiatrists or social workers *should be involved* not only in assigning the baby a specific gender, but in the child's upbringing. Modern treatment options include corrective surgery, hormone therapy, peer support and counselling. Today, families with DSD children can generally get the help they need to make a determination regarding the sex of the baby, along with on-going help for the child. *This has **not** always been the case however.*

I cannot ***even begin to understand*** what some of these children go through growing up. If these biological conditions were not already difficult enough, add to this the ***secrecy and shame*** that will often accompany these conditions. For some of these children, the biggest problem with being intersex is not abnormal body parts, it is the **isolation** and invisibility. It is not hard for them to feel like a *freak* of nature. Parents sometimes keep things like this "hush hush" because of their *own* shame or misguided guilt. These parents need to remember that it is not about *what's best for them*, it is about ***what's best for the child!*** I would encourage parents of these children, in addition to seeking the above mentioned support, to also seek out ***spiritual support and guidance***. Some parents get *mad at God* because of these things. Although I cannot explain *why* these birth abnormalities (and other *horrible* things) happen to **innocent** children...I can tell everyone ***with absolute certainty***, **"GOD had nothing to do with it"**. Some of these infants may not be clearly male or female at birth, but they *are* clearly human! *We* must never forget that. They deserve to be loved and cared for ***as God did intend,*** and not judged or ridiculed. God certainly did not intend for these individuals to be told by anyone, ***especially*** Christian believers, that their choices are fueled by lust...not biology.

Chapter 7

The Apology

Previous chapters of this book discuss about how *certain* homosexuals were born different from other people. Chapter 4 offers one possible Biblical explanation as to why they have always felt different, and introduces a revelation from the Scriptures regarding a *divine destiny* given to certain special individuals (We will talk more about this destiny in chapter 8). Chapter 5 discusses how difficult it is dealing with one's sexuality...particularly if one believes him/herself to be homosexual. Chapter 5 also discusses how satan will attack the gifted individuals from chapter 4, trying to rob him or her of their God-given purpose by lying to him or her. Chapter 6 talks about those who have been born with biological reasons for being different. These previous chapters, although *written for everyone to read*, will **not apply** to everyone. Until now, this book is *applicable* for the Christian community as a whole, but only for a select group of the LGBT community. This chapter however, while still being applicable to Christians...both fake or real, will be applicable for **ALL** members of the LGBT community. This chapter differs from previous chapters in that it **applies to everyone.** If you are a member of the LGBT community, you have experienced **prejudice and judgmentalism** at one point or another (These things were discussed in detail in chapter 3). In order for this chapter to have a fuller meaning, one needs to have read chapter 3 and be agreeable to it's conclusions. No one **has to agree** with everything written in chapter 3, ***but it will sure make reading this chapter all whole lot more fun!***

If you haven't figured it out by now, I am heterosexual. Because I am heterosexual, I cannot begin to tell any homosexual that I know what he or she is going through, or that I understand how he or she feels. If you are reading this book, and a practicing homosexual, I pray that you take this chapter to heart. Regardless of how you believe God did, or did not, make you...**you are loved by God**. God is love (1st John 4:8). He may not agree with everything that we do, but that does not set aside His love for us. "For God so loved the world, that he gave his only begotten Son, that whosoever shall believeth in Him shall not perish, but have everlasting life" John 3:16 (King James Version). Homosexuals are *in the world;* therefore, God loves them...and if He loves them, why shouldn't we? One can still love somebody and talk to him or her about a behavior believed to be wrong...**just do it in a way that is not judgmental or critical.** Present your concern in a way that does not come off as being arrogant or "holier than thou". The penalty for all sin is equal in God's eyes, so why do some people make certain sins more wrong than others? It is interesting to note, that there **are** a few sins mentioned in the Bible that God *especially hates*. At the top of His list is pride! I find this extremely ironic because the spirit that generally governs judgmentalism *is pride*. In some instances, the people who believe they are *straightening out* someone else's sin, are actually committing the sin that sets on top of God's hate list.

Let's assume for a moment for the purposes of this chapter (go with me here), that homosexuality is a sin. What makes this sin any greater than any other sin in God's eyes? People choose every day to go against God's plans and break His commandments. As discussed in Chapter 3, even if a person is wrong in their belief, they still have **the right to be wrong**. Just as I have my right to choose my sexual orientation and preferences, all members of the LGBT community have their rights (and reasons) for choosing their sexual orientation and preferences. Yet, I believe homosexuality to be the ***number one talked about sin in the world***...public enemy number one for *some churches!* I am certainly not trying to downgrade the seriousness of **any** sin, including homosexuality, but I am trying to ask the world (outside of the homosexual community) why it is that people are so judgemental and critical towards homosexuals? When was the last time anyone saw a person standing outside of the courthouse holding up a picket sign protesting gluttony? When was the last time someone saw a sign that said, "All persons that cheat on their taxes will burn in hell"? What about hate crimes? Has anyone ever heard of someone being "beat up" because he or she *was obese?*

It is truly unfortunate that all of this criticism and judgmentalism takes place. More unfortunate however, is the fact that no one does a better job at judging homosexuals than people from the Christian community. In every church I have ever attended, I have overheard judgmental statements concerning homosexuals. There are also members in my own family who are highly critical of homosexuality. Again, I am not justifying any behavior that *God calls* sinful, I am questioning however, "Why this particular topic fuels so much fire?"

As I stated above, I cannot begin to understand what the average homosexual in America goes through. I live in a small midwestern town. Although this town *claims* to be tolerant and trendsetting in its standards, in practice, this city is very judgmental. Please understand that I am not speaking about everyone. There are Christians (and non-Christians) everywhere who are genuinely sincere in their beliefs, who (from a true heart) love all people...including those practicing homosexuality! These individuals are not judgmental or critical. Many devout Christians pray every day, asking God to help those struggling with their sexuality. These *show* love, not just with words, but with their *deeds*. Unfortunately, these are not the *majority*...these believers are the *minority*. The judgmental majority (for the most part) do not know their own Bible, nor do they (in many instances) know why they believe the way they do. Some believe this way because, "Grandpa believed that way". Others believe because, "That's what pastor teaches". Some believe the way they do because their parents taught them that way. Regardless of the beliefs someone has been subjected to, if that person is a true Christian, he or she will endeavor to be led by the Spirit of God and follow *what the Bible teaches...not what man teaches!*

This brings me to the focal point of this chapter...**the APOLOGY.** Yes, I want to offer an apology to *all* members of the LGBT community on behalf of myself and Christians everywhere. In fact, I wish to apologize on behalf of any person who has bigoted him/herself and wrongly judged you. **I humbly ask forgiveness for our wrongful judgements**...particularly if you happen to be one of those select few discussed in chapter 4 (who have been given the gift of celibacy) or one of those discussed in chapter 6 (who were born with physical abnormalities). In addition, if you *are* a member of one of these two categories, I offer you **"two"** apologies. One for judging your previous sexual choices, and one for not knowing who you were born to be.

For those gifted with celibacy from birth, **please forgive our ignorance**. Even Christians (who *claim* to know the Bible) have not understood what the Bible says about you! We did not know about your special gift from God, nor why you are truly different. *We failed you* by being unable, *through ignorance,* to provide the *truth* for your questions. When you asked "Why did God make me this way?" and "Why have I always been different?" we judged you. Instead of telling you "God *did not* make you homosexual, but *He did* make you **different** by giving you the gift of celibacy" we accused you of "lying to yourself" and being deceived. When in fact, you *were* telling the truth. Although you yourselves did not know about the gift that had been given you, you *did know* that you were different. You asked for answers, but were judged instead. You wanted help, but received criticism instead. You needed to be lifted up, but were cut down instead with statements like, "God made them Adam and Eve, not Adam and Steve". **Dear God, please forgive us!** You are precious in the eyes of God and were granted an amazing gift. You have a unique calling to achieve greatness in the kingdom of God, yet we have judged and ridiculed you. Please, find it in your heart to **FORGIVE** us. *We have been truly ignorant;* thinking you to be *gay,* you have been in reality *gifted*.

For those who were born with defects or abnormalities, **please forgive our ignorance as well**. Rather than take the time to listen to you, we made assumptions. Rather than get all of the facts we judged. We did not know about your biological reasons for being different. *We failed you also,* by being unable...*through ignorance*...to provide the truth for your questions. When you asked, "Why did God allow this to happen to me?" and "Why did He make me like this?" we judged you. Instead of telling you, "God did not make you like this and He loves you regardless of how you were born" we closed our eyes to your difficulties. You too asked for answers...but were judged instead. You wanted help...but were rejected instead. You needed to be lifted up...but were cut down instead with statements like, "God has His reasons, your parents must have sinned or done something wrong". **Dear God, please forgive us!** You are precious in the eyes of God and **NOT** a mistake! You too are unique and have a special opportunity to serve in the kingdom of God by helping others like yourself...2nd Corinthians 1:4: (God) who comforts us in our afflictions *so that we will be able to comfort others who are in **similar** afflictions* using the same comfort with which we ourselves have been comforted with by God (Translation mine). Please, find it in your heart to **FORGIVE** us. *We have been truly ignorant;* thinking you to be *gay,* you have been in reality *a gift*.

Chapter 8

The Destiny

In this final chapter I want to share some Scriptures that I believe strongly apply to the individuals this book is dedicated to, with regards *to their calling*...their ***destiny***. Hopefully, these Bible verses will also serve to **encourage** those individuals who were born differently from the rest of us. Everyone, including those who are different, even *abnormal*, have a divine destiny. There is a purpose for all of us being here, and why we are who we are. I believe in order to be truly successful, each person should seek out their divine destiny and do everything within his or her power to fulfill it. The world's definition of success is certainly different from that of God's. People can be selfish, critical, and certainly judgmental...***but God is not.*** It is my hope and prayer that this final chapter will, along with the other chapters, significantly touch the hearts of those who are born different, and help *open the eyes* of the rest of us.

David writes in Psalm 139:13 says, "I will give thanks to you because I have been so amazingly and miraculously made. Your works are miraculous, and my soul is fully aware of this" (God's Word Translation). David was the first King of Isreal chosen by God. Although David was a King, his life was very difficult and filled with horrendous trials. Yet, he was still ***thankful*** to God because he realized what each one of us should realize, that **we are all miracles**. Human beings, even those who are born different, are still amazing. In the New Testament, 1st Peter 2:9 states, "But you are a chosen race, a royal priesthood, a holy nation, a people for God's own possession, that you may proclaim the excellence of him who called you out of darkness into his marvelous light" (World English Bible). What *better way* to proclaim the excellency of God than to choose to rise above the accusations, the judgments, and the difficulties associated with being born different and fulfill your God given destiny! No matter what the world may say, you are not an accident, or a mistake. Even if your *own* **parents** *forsake you*, God *will* care for you. Psalm 27:10, says, "Even if my father and mother abandon me, the LORD cares for me" (Holman Standard Christian Bible).

I cannot tell you specifically what God has planned for your life. *Personally,* I do not believe that God would want me to tell you even *if* I knew. I somewhat think He wants each of us to work it out **individually** (for ourselves) with Him. **Sometimes the journey is required to prepare us for the destination**. I *can* share with you however, what He tells *all* of us through the prophet Jeremiah. In chapter 29, verse 11 God says, "For I know the plans I have for you," declares the LORD, "plans to prosper you and not to harm you, plans to give you hope and a future" (New International Version). I do not know how much plainer He could spell it out for us. God has a wonderful plan for our lives. Yes, hardships and tragedies occur. Horrible things happen to good people every day, but God is **not** the one doing it. Many will not fulfill their God-given destiny, but they will not have God to blame for it. **God has done his part**. You are here, you are reading this book, and you have breath; therefore, you have a chance.

Understandably, there are those who wonder (even after reading this book) how God could ever use them. Not just people from the LGBT community either. Many people wonder why God would choose them for *ministry* work. First of all, everyone should realize the word "minister" in the English versions of the Bible translates literally as "servant", and we are all called to be servants. In fact, 2nd Corinthians 5:20 states: "We are ambassadors for Christ, as though God were making an appeal through us..." (New American Standard Bible). One does not have to be a pastor, preacher, Bible study graduate, college graduate, evangelist, Sunday school teacher, seminary graduate, church elder, deacon, apostle, or prophet to be a minister (servant) for God. One just needs to be ***willing to serve***.

The Scriptures do provide some *clues* for the answer to the above questions. God wants above all else for His creation to know **He is real** and that **He cares for us**. Take for example the book of Ezekiel. The phrase "and you shall know that I am the LORD" occurs 65 times in this book of the Bible. I believe God was trying to make a point. He is aware however, that we *sometimes* need to actually "see" some things in order for us to believe and have faith. This helps explain why often times God chooses people who *"in the eyes of society"* are **nobodies**. He specifically picks people in many instances *because* they **do not have** talent or special abilities! He does this deliberately, so that when people witness the amazing things these individuals are able to accomplish, they are driven to accept the fact that there ***must*** be a God. He uses *nobodies* to confound the *somebodies*. 1st Corinthians 1:26-29 tells us, "Think about the circumstances of your call, brothers and sisters. Not many were wise by human standards, not many were powerful, not many were born to a privileged position. But God chose what the world thinks foolish to shame the wise, and God chose what the world thinks weak to shame the strong. God chose what is low and despised in the world, what is regarded as nothing, to set aside what is regarded as something, so that no one can boast in His presence (NET Translation). How awesome; ***what society rejects...God accepts, and uses!***

Now that we have discussed the "why me" part of the destiny, let's talk about the "where". The **where to begin** part is really something you will have to *ask God about specifically*. However, the Bible does provide us with a couple of clues. In 2nd Corinthians 10:13-15, we learn that we each have a God given "measure of influence" or "sphere" that we are responsible for. We are *where we are,* for a reason also. There is an old saying, "grow where you are planted". We discussed earlier in this book how God desires for us to help others who are in situations which we have experienced ourselves (2nd Corinthians 1:4). It makes good sense. Who better to help someone through a divorce, than someone who has been through a divorce? Who better to help someone work through the pain of losing a child, than someone who has lost a child? In the same way, who better to help someone *struggling with their sexual identity,* than someone who has worked through it themselves? Who better to help someone growing up with genital ambiguity, than an adult who has **overcome** their sexual issues, and worked through the shame?

In closing, let us cover the "*how*" part of the destiny...as in "how do I get started?" Ironically, you have **already** taken the first step...*having read this book*. There was something **inside of you** that moved you to buy this book and read it. Perhaps a question that needed answered, or maybe an *emptiness* in your heart that needed filled? Regardless of what it was, I **doubt** that it was simply curiosity. The first thing I would recommend to everyone would be **to pray**. If you already know God, and believe His word then you know how to pray. If you do not believe in God however, or have *any* spiritual beliefs for that matter, I would encourage you to perform a very heartfelt and sincere **self inventory**. Is all of this just a coincidence? Or perhaps, *could* there really be a God who cares about me? If you come to believe that God is real, then I can answer the "caring about you" part myself. **Yes, He is real...and He cares**. Here is how *I know*. There is *NO way* that I would ever consider writing a book like this if I didn't believe 100% that there was a God, and that part of *my destiny* was to **write this book!** I am certainly not out for attention or recognition, prominence or money, but I do wish to fulfill my God-given destiny...a destiny which *for me* includes writing this book. Whether or not you agree with what is written in this book is entirely up to you. The fact is, you did **choose** to read it. This was **no accident**. I challenge each of you to take the time to pray and have the courage to ask God about this book. Whether you believe it or not, we each have a divine destiny. I realize that for many this book will have no special meaning, but I also realize for a select few this book could change their lives. I hope you are the latter.

About the author:

Garris and and wife live in a small midwestern town in the United States. They are both active church members who share a desire to help others, particularly those who are labeled by society. Garris teaches Sunday school at his local church and does part-time prison ministry. He has been a Christian for 26 years and enjoys reading and studying the Bible.

www.ingramcontent.com/pod-product-compliance
Lightning Source LLC
Chambersburg PA
CBHW031008090426
42737CB00008B/734